Shadows Over the Socialscape

Unmasking Power and Ideology Through Adorno's Lens

The Curious Philosopher

Copyright Page

Disclaimer

The views and opinions expressed in this book are those of the author(s) and do not necessarily reflect the official policy or position of any other agency, organization, employer, or company. The contents of this book are for informational and educational purposes only and are not intended to serve as professional advice, diagnosis, or treatment.

The information provided in this book is believed to be accurate and reliable as of the date of publication. However, it may include some errors or inaccuracies, and no warranty or guarantee is provided regarding the accuracy, timeliness, or applicability of the content.

Readers are encouraged to consult with professional philosophers, educators, or other qualified professionals where appropriate for personalized advice. The author(s) and publisher shall not be liable for any loss, damage, or harm caused or alleged to be caused, directly or indirectly, by the information or ideas contained, suggested, or referenced in this book.

By reading this book, the reader acknowledges and agrees that they are solely responsible for how they interpret and apply the information contained herein.

This book may also include references to other works, studies, and sources. These references are provided for further reading and exploration and do not imply endorsement or validation of the specific theories, viewpoints, or interpretations presented in those works.

Introduction

In a world bustling with myriad noises, from the roaring engines of capitalism to the soft whispers of daily life, there was a thinker named Theodor W. Adorno who sought to tune into the deeper, often unheard rhythms that shape our society. Born in Frankfurt, Germany, in 1903, Adorno was a philosopher, a sociologist, and a composer, whose work revolved around trying to understand the complex machinery operating beneath the surface of our social and cultural lives. Much like a detective solving a mind-boggling mystery, Adorno sought to unveil the hidden scripts directing the drama of human existence.

Now, you might wonder, why does this matter? Imagine a theater where a play unfolds. The actors follow a script, the lights set a mood, and the audience reacts. Yet, the script isn't written by the actors, nor is the scene set by them. There's a larger force at work — the director, the scriptwriter, and the cultural norms that they all operate within. Adorno believed that similar forces shape our society. His philosophical lens helps us see the strings of power and ideologies pulling at every aspect of our lives, much like a puppeteer manipulating a puppet.

Enter the realm of 'critical theory,' a tool Adorno and his colleagues developed to dissect the unseen mechanics of society. Critical theory is akin to possessing a magical lens that helps us see the invisible — the underlying beliefs, power dynamics, and structures that shape our actions, reactions, and interactions. It's about unveiling the hidden scripts, questioning the status quo, and exploring the spaces where change can be seeded.

The stage for our exploration in this book is set. Through Adorno's lens, we aim to unravel the fabric of societal norms, shedding light on the often unseen but powerful forces that shape our collective experience. Our journey will delve into the heart of modern culture, exposing the contradictions that lie within and the potential for change that bubbles beneath the surface. This isn't merely an academic expedition but a quest for understanding that concerns us all. As we flip through the pages of Adorno's critical theory, we'll explore how it enables us to question, to challenge, and to envision a world less bound by unseen strings of control.

Our objective is clear: to unveil the chains of ideologies and power structures that shape our existence and to explore the avenues of change that lie within our grasp. Through Adorno's insightful lens, we hope to foster a conversation about the unseen forces that dictate our lives and how we might begin to tug back at the strings that bind us. So, as we step into the labyrinth of Adorno's thought, let's keep our eyes wide open, ready to question and to be questioned, for within the maze lies the promise of understanding and the spark of change.

Chapter One: Laying the Groundwork

Before delving into the heart of Theodor Adorno's insights, it's essential to understand the soil from which his ideas sprouted. Let's travel back in time to a period where traditional ways of thinking were being questioned and new ideas were taking root. This journey takes us to the realm of 'critical theory,' a school of thought that aimed to understand and challenge the social structures shaping our world.

The Birth of Critical Theory

Imagine a group of thinkers coming together, united by a common dissatisfaction with the prevailing social and philosophical ideas of their time. They believed that much of the existing thinking was like wearing rose-colored glasses, ignoring the less pleasant realities of society. This group aimed to take off these glasses and see society as it truly was, warts and all. This was the birth of 'critical theory,' a way of looking at the world that sought to understand and critique the societal structures that hold power and perpetuate injustices.

The Frankfurt School: A Melting Pot of Minds

The intellectual home of critical theory was a place known as the Frankfurt School, founded in the early 20th century in Germany. This wasn't a school in the traditional sense, but rather a gathering of like-minded intellectuals who were keen on exploring the societal forces at play. Among these thinkers was our protagonist, Theodor Adorno. The Frankfurt School was like a cauldron where ideas bubbled, mixed, and brewed. It was a space that allowed Adorno and his contemporaries to question and critique the status quo.

Adorno's Core Principles: Unveiling the Hidden Scripts

Now, onto the man of the hour, Theodor Adorno. His approach to critical theory was akin to peeling layers off an onion to reveal what's hidden beneath. Let's break down his core ideas into simple nuggets:

The Culture Industry: Adorno argued that culture - the music we listen to, the films we watch, the art we consume - isn't merely a source of enjoyment. It's an industry that shapes our desires, attitudes, and behaviors, often in the service of powerful interests.

Negative Dialectics: Adorno encouraged us to embrace contradiction and to question apparent harmonies. By doing this, we could expose the underlying issues within society and strive for a deeper understanding.

Aesthetics as Critique: For Adorno, art and aesthetics weren't just about beauty. They were tools to critique society and to imagine alternatives.

Autonomy and Emancipation: Adorno believed in the potential for individuals to break free from societal shackles, but this required recognizing and challenging the unseen forces at play.

Our stage is set, and the actors are ready. With Adorno's insights as our guide, we're about to embark on a journey into the depths of society's structures. As we venture further, we'll delve deeper into these core principles, exploring the ways they help unveil the scripts dictating our lives and the potential they hold for scripting new narratives. Through this journey, we'll begin to see the world through Adorno's eyes - a world full of unseen forces, waiting to be discovered, questioned, and perhaps, reimagined.

Chapter Two: The Culture Industry Revisited

Imagine living in a town where every shop, every restaurant, every theater was owned by the same person. Now, what if that person decided to paint every building pink, play the same song on loop, and serve only vanilla ice cream? The choices of the town's inhabitants would be swayed by the whims of this one individual, right? Theodor Adorno saw our cultural landscape similarly, dominated by few but impacting all. He coined this domination as the "Culture Industry."

Unveiling the 'Culture Industry'

The Culture Industry isn't about factories churning out paintings or songs; it's about how the world of entertainment, media, and art isn't as free and diverse as we might think. Adorno believed that much of what we see, hear, and enjoy is manufactured by a system aimed at maintaining certain power structures and ideologies. In simpler terms, the songs we hum, the movies we adore, and the trends we follow are often served to us from a limited menu, while we're made to believe it's a grand buffet.

Mass Culture: A Silent Conductor

Let's dive a bit deeper. Mass culture, the popular stuff we all like, plays a significant role in shaping our beliefs, desires, and behaviors. It's like a silent conductor orchestrating a symphony of societal attitudes. For instance, when films repeatedly portray a certain gender or race in a stereotypical manner, they reinforce and perpetuate existing prejudices. Similarly, when advertisements showcase an endless parade of consumer goods, they fuel a culture of materialism.

The Real-World Script of the Culture Industry

Let's bring Adorno's idea to life with some real-world examples:

Music Industry: Ever notice how a lot of pop music sounds similar? The industry often prioritizes catchy, formulaic tunes that guarantee success over unique, challenging compositions.

Film and Television: From Hollywood to Netflix, the stories often uphold certain ideologies. For instance, the glorification of wealth, the idealization of certain body types, or the reinforcement of gender roles.

Advertising: Ads don't just sell products; they sell lifestyles and ideals. They create desires, making us want things we didn't even know we needed.

Social Media: Platforms like Instagram and TikTok often become echo chambers where the same types of content, ideas, and aesthetics are recycled, shaping our preferences and perceptions.

Through these examples, we can see the Culture Industry at work, subtly molding our tastes, opinions, and behaviors. It's like a tide that sweeps us along a predetermined course, often without us even realizing it.

As we journey through the realm of the Culture Industry, Adorno's insights act like a compass, helping us navigate the often unseen, unspoken influences that shape our cultural landscape. With every tune we hum or movie we watch, we're not just engaging with a piece of art, but a piece of a larger narrative scripted by the Culture Industry. This chapter uncovers just the tip of the iceberg, prompting us to question and explore the unseen forces that shape our collective narrative and individual stories.

Chapter Three: Negative Dialectics and Social Contradictions

Imagine a room full of people who always agree with each other, echoing the same thoughts, over and over again. It might feel harmonious but also stagnant and unchallenging. Now, what if someone enters the room and starts questioning the common consensus? This person might stir the pot, bring in new perspectives, and ignite a spark for deeper understanding among the group. This scenario mirrors the essence of what Theodor Adorno referred to as 'negative dialectics.'

The Dance of Negative Dialectics

Negative dialectics is like a dance of thought where instead of moving smoothly to a melody of agreements, we stumble upon discord, question harmony, and engage with the rhythm of contradiction. In simpler terms, it's about not taking things at face value but delving deeper to uncover hidden truths, often revealing conflicting aspects within society.

Unmasking Social Contradictions

When we apply this method of questioning and examining contradictions to society, we unveil layers of issues that often lurk beneath a facade of harmony. For example, a country might proclaim equality for all, but a closer look could reveal systemic discrimination against certain groups. This dissonance, between what's professed and what's practiced, is a social contradiction. Adorno's negative dialectics urge us to identify and engage with these contradictions, not shy away from them.

Real-world Reflections of Contradictions

Let's bring this into the real world with some examples:

Wealth Disparity: Societies often herald the narrative of meritocracy, yet the stark wealth disparity reveals a contradiction. The idea that anyone can "make it" clashes with the reality of systemic barriers.

Gender Equality: Many societies claim to uphold gender equality, yet discrepancies in pay, representation, and societal expectations unveil a contradiction between principle and practice.

Freedom of Expression: The principle of free speech is championed, yet instances of censorship, silencing dissent, or propagating fake news reveal a conflicting narrative.

Through the lens of negative dialectics, these contradictions are not mere problems, but invitations to dig deeper, to question, and to understand the structures that perpetuate such discrepancies.

As we venture through Adorno's realm of negative dialectics, we're encouraged to embrace the uncomfortable, to question the seemingly unquestionable, and to unearth the contradictions that reside within social norms and ideologies. It's a journey that doesn't just expose the fissures, but also invites us to envision a society that is more reflective, more aware, and perhaps, more just. Adorno's negative dialectics is not a pessimistic resignation to social woes, but a hopeful call for awareness, engagement, and ultimately, transformation.

Chapter Four: Aesthetics as Social Critique

Imagine walking through a bustling city, surrounded by skyscrapers and billboards, when you stumble upon a mural. This isn't just any mural; it depicts a powerful scene of social justice, evoking emotions and thoughts about the world around you. Suddenly, the city feels different, doesn't it? This is the transformative power of art, a core element of Adorno's philosophy that we're about to delve into.

Painting Ideas with Aesthetic Theory

Adorno believed that art and aesthetics aren't just about creating or appreciating beautiful things. They're about challenging the way we see and interact with the world. Through art, we can critique society, exposing its flaws and envisioning new possibilities. Adorno's aesthetic theory is like handing artists a brush not just to paint pictures, but to paint ideas, question norms, and stir the societal pot.

The Dual Role of Art and Aesthetics

Art can be both a mirror and a window. It reflects the prevailing ideologies of society, sometimes reinforcing them. For example, a movie glorifying war might reinforce nationalist ideologies. On the flip side, art can also challenge these ideologies. A novel depicting the struggles of a marginalized group might open windows to new perspectives and foster empathy.

Revolutionary Canvas: Case Studies Through Adornian Lens

Let's explore some real-world examples to understand the revolutionary potential of art:

Banksy's Street Art: The elusive artist Banksy uses street art to critique various social and political issues. His murals often spark conversations about power, inequality, and the human condition.

The "Guernica" by Pablo Picasso: This iconic painting is a powerful anti-war statement, reflecting the horrors of the Bombing of Guernica during the Spanish Civil War.

The #MeToo Movement: Though not a traditional art form, the storytelling at the heart of the #MeToo movement challenged prevailing narratives about sexual harassment and assault, creating a global dialogue.

Through these case studies, we see how art transcends aesthetic appeal to provoke thought, challenge norms, and even catalyze social change. Through Adorno's lens, every stroke of paint, every line of poetry, and every note of music can be a ripple in the waters of societal norms and ideologies.

As we explore Adorno's aesthetic theory, we learn to see beyond the surface, to appreciate the depth of critique, the boldness of challenge, and the potential for transformation that art and aesthetics can offer.

Our journey through the realm of aesthetics isn't just an exploration of art, but an exploration of the ideas that shape, challenge, and sometimes even disrupt the social narrative. It's about realizing that every piece of art holds the potential to be more than just a beautiful object, but a catalyst for thought, discussion, and even change.

Chapter Five: The Possibility of Change

Imagine standing at the edge of a dense forest, knowing that through it lies a path to a sunlit clearing. The journey may be tough, filled with brambles and unknowns, but the promise of reaching that clearing fuels your steps. This imagery encapsulates the essence of change within Adorno's framework. It's about navigating through the thicket of societal norms and power structures, towards a clearing of awareness and transformation.

Navigating Change Through Adorno's Lens

Adorno's philosophy doesn't just expose the chains that bind society; it also hints at the keys that could unlock them. Change, according to him, begins with awareness — the ability to see beyond the facade, to question, and to critique. And this awareness is not a solitary endeavor but a collective awakening, challenging the status quo and envisioning alternatives.

Catalysts of Change: The Intellectual and The Artist

In the theater of social change, Adorno casts intellectuals and artists in starring roles. They are the torchbearers illuminating the unseen, the unheard, and the unspoken. Through critique and creative expression, they can challenge prevailing narratives, spark dialogue, and pave the way for societal reflection and transformation.

Echoes of Adorno in the Real World

Let's explore some real-world movements that resonate with Adorno's call for social transformation:

Black Lives Matter Movement: This movement challenges systemic racism, echoes Adorno's call to unveil and address societal contradictions.

Climate Change Activism: Activists like Greta Thunberg, through intellectual critique and public engagement, embody the spirit of challenging established norms, much in line with Adorno's philosophy.

The Arab Spring: This wave of protests across the Middle East and North Africa was a stark demonstration of collective awakening and the quest for social transformation, resonating with Adorno's ideas on change.

These movements highlight the ripple effect of individual and collective awareness, critique, and action in challenging and changing the prevailing narratives.

As we stand on the precipice of understanding, with a vista of societal norms and power structures stretched out before us, Adorno's philosophy offers a compass to navigate the path of change. It invites us to question, to challenge, and to imagine a world where the brambles of injustice and ignorance are cleared, making way for a clearing of enlightenment and transformation. Through the lens of Adorno's critical theory, we're not just observers but active participants in the narrative of social change, each with a role to play in scripting a story of awareness, critique, and hopefully, a better tomorrow.

Chapter Six: Adorno in the Modern Context

As we step back into the bustling reality of today's world, armed with the insights from Adorno's philosophical voyage, we find ourselves in a landscape that, although decades apart from Adorno's time, still echoes with the resonance of his theories. The stage has changed, but the script of power structures and ideological impositions remains strikingly familiar. Let's journey through the modern context, exploring how Adorno's critical theory illuminates the path amidst the new challenges and opportunities that define our era.

Adorno's Echo in Today's World

Adorno's critical theory is like a timeless lens that sharpens our view of the contemporary world. The culture industry has morphed into a digital giant, where social media and streaming platforms dictate the rhythm of societal discourse. The call for critical examination of societal norms and ideologies rings true now, perhaps more than ever, as we navigate the complex waters of globalization, digitalization, and social justice movements.

Modern-day Giants: Power and Ideology in the Digital Age

Today's power structures and ideological impositions have taken on new avatars. The digital realm is a powerful player, shaping our perceptions, interactions, and even our democracies. Meanwhile, the ideological battles of our time play out not just in parliaments and town halls, but also in tweets and hashtags.

Engaging with Adorno: Critiques and Expansions

Adorno's theories continue to spark dialogue, with modern thinkers both critiquing and building upon his ideas. Some argue that his notions of the culture industry and negative dialectics need a re-tuning to accommodate the digital, decentralized nature of modern cultural and social exchanges. Others find a wealth of inspiration in Adorno's aesthetic theory, applying it to new forms of art and social critique that blossom in the digital age.

Bridging Past and Present: A Conversation Across Time

Our exploration doesn't stop here. Adorno's critical theory invites us to engage in a continuous dialogue, to question, critique, and reimagine the structures that shape our world. It's a conversation that bridges the past and present, offering a rich tapestry of insights to navigate the challenges and opportunities that lie ahead.

The modern context is both a testament to the enduring relevance of Adorno's critical theory and a call for its continual evolution. As we step into the unfolding narrative of the 21st century, Adorno's philosophy holds a mirror to the evolving face of society, urging us to keep questioning, keep challenging, and keep striving for a deeper understanding of the world we inhabit. Through the lens of Adorno's critical theory, we're not merely spectators but active players in the unfolding drama of societal transformation, each with a vital part to play in scripting the narrative of change.

Conclusion

As we step off the philosophical boat steered by Theodor Adorno's thoughts, we find ourselves on the shores of reflection, with a treasure trove of insights that promise to illuminate the path as we navigate the social and cultural landscape of our times. Our journey through the waves of critical theory, the storms of societal contradictions, and the calm waters of aesthetic critique has enriched our understanding, urging us to look beyond the facade of social phenomena and delve into the core that shapes them.

The Compass of Critical Theory

Adorno's critical theory emerged as a compass, enabling us to discern the often invisible forces of power and ideology that steer the societal ship. From the culture industry's subtle script to the potential of negative dialectics in unveiling social contradictions, Adorno's philosophy invites us to question, critique, and imagine.

The Art of Seeing Differently

Adorno championed the role of art and the intellectual in painting a vivid picture of societal norms, challenging the status quo, and envisioning a canvas of change. His aesthetic theory opened the doors to viewing art not merely as a form of beauty, but as a potent form of social critique.

The Imperative for Critical Examination

In a world that often favors the comfort of conformity, Adorno's philosophy is a clarion call for critical examination. It's an invitation to not just passively exist within societal structures but to actively engage with them, question them, and strive for a deeper understanding that paves the way for social change.

Stepping Forward with Adorno's Insights

As we stand at the precipice of modern-day challenges, the essence of Adorno's critical theory echoes through time, urging us to harness the power of critical analysis in our pursuit of social change. It's about fostering a culture of questioning that disrupts complacency and sparks a flame of transformation.

With Adorno's critical theory as our guide, we are better equipped to decode the complex narratives of power and ideology that shape our world. As we step forward, each stride is a step towards not just understanding the world as it is, but imagining the world as it could be.

Our journey through Adorno's philosophical landscape is not an end, but a beginning. A beginning of a lifelong engagement with the world around us, an ongoing quest for understanding, and a continuous endeavor towards envisioning and forging a path towards a more just, reflective, and enlightened society. And as we step into the world, with a fresh lens of understanding, we carry with us the essence of Adorno's message: the power of critical thought in unveiling the unseen, challenging the accepted, and nurturing the seeds of change.

About The Curious Philosopher

Welcome to The Curious Philosopher, your dedicated platform for diving deep into the world of philosophy. We are more than just a YouTube channel or a book publisher. We are a beacon of enlightenment, making complex philosophical concepts accessible and engaging for all.

Our YouTube channel is a rich repository of philosophy made simple. We take the profound and often complex ideas from the world of philosophy and break them down into digestible, easy-to-understand content. From the ancient wisdom of Socrates to the existentialist thoughts of Sartre, we cover a broad spectrum of philosophical schools and thoughts, making philosophy accessible to everyone, regardless of their background or prior knowledge.

As a book publisher, we take the same approach, transforming intricate philosophical theories into comprehensible narratives. Our books are not just collections of words, but vessels of wisdom that make philosophy approachable and relatable. We believe that philosophy should not be confined to academic circles, but should be available to all who seek to understand the world and their place in it.

At The Curious Philosopher, we believe in the power of curiosity and the pursuit of knowledge. We are here to stoke the fires of your curiosity, to guide you on your intellectual journey, and to help you navigate the fascinating world of philosophy.

If you are someone who is not afraid to question, to explore, and to learn, then you are in the right place. Join us on this journey of exploration, as we make philosophy easy to understand, one concept at a time.

Be sure to visit our Youtube channel at:

https://www.curiousphilosopher.com/youtube

You can also visit us on the web at

https://www.curiousphilosopher.com

Welcome to The Curious Philosopher. Stay curious. Stay enlightened.